RICHARD M. Nixon

RICHARD M. *Nixon*

OUR THIRTY-SEVENTH PRESIDENT

By Ann Graham Gaines

SPIRIT
of America™

The Child's World®, Inc.
Chanhassen, Minnesota

6

RICHARD M. *Nixon*

Published in the United States of America by The Child's World®, Inc.
PO Box 326 • Chanhassen, MN 55317-0326 • 800-599-READ • www.childsworld.com

Acknowledgments

The Creative Spark: Mary Francis-DeMarois, Project Director; Elizabeth Sirimarco Budd, Series Editor; Robert Court, Design and Art Direction; Janine Graham, Page Layout; Jennifer Moyers, Production

The Child's World®, Inc.: Mary Berendes, Publishing Director; Red Line Editorial, Fact Research; Cindy Klingel, Curriculum Advisor; Robert Noyed, Historical Advisor

Photos

Cover: White House Collection, courtesy White House Historical Association; Corbis: 30, 31, 32, 33, 35; Dwight D. Eisenhower Library, Abilene, Texas: 20; John Fitzgerald Kennedy Library, Boston, MA: 22; Gerald R. Ford Presidential Library: 37; Library of Congress: 21, 23, 27, 29; National Archives: 12, 13, 24, 28, 36; Courtesy of Whittier College: 7, 9, 10, 11, 14, 15, 16, 19

Registration

The Child's World®, Inc., Spirit of America™, and their associated logos are the sole property and registered trademarks of The Child's World®, Inc.

Library of Congress Cataloging-in-Publication Data

Gaines, Ann.
    Richard M. Nixon : our thirty-seventh president / by Ann Graham Gaines.
        p. cm.
    Includes bibliographical references (p.) and index.
    ISBN 1–56766–871–2 (lib. bdg. : alk. paper)
    1. Nixon, Richard M. (Richard Milhous), 1913–   —Juvenile literature. 2. Presidents—United States—Biography—Juvenile literature. [1. Nixon, Richard M. (Richard Milhous), 1913– 2. Presidents.]   I. Title.
    E856 .G34 2001
    973.924'092--dc21

                                                    00-013166

10   30   35

Contents

Chapter ONE

Young Nixon

Richard M. Nixon rose from a humble background to become America's 37th president. "I believe in the American dream because I have seen it come true in my own life," he once said.

IN 1974, RICHARD NIXON BECAME THE FIRST president of the United States to **resign** from office. He stepped down from the presidency when it became clear that he would be impeached. When the House of Representatives votes to impeach, it charges the president with a crime or serious misdeed. President Nixon was in trouble because of his role in a burglary. In the burglary, papers were stolen from the office of Nixon's political enemies. Today Americans know he tried to cover up the theft. Even so, some remember Nixon as an important leader.

Richard Milhous Nixon was born on January 9, 1913, in Yorba Linda, California. His parents were Frank and Hannah Nixon. Over the years, Frank Nixon worked at many jobs. He was a streetcar driver, a farmer, and then a grocer. By nature, he was an angry man who liked to argue. His main interest was politics, the work of the government. Hannah Nixon was a housewife who took good care of her family. She was a quiet, patient, and religious woman who influenced her children a great deal. When Richard was born, he had one older brother, Harold. Later the Nixons had three more sons, Donald, Arthur, and Edward.

The family lived in Yorba Linda for 10 years. They built a house there and planted a grove of lemon trees. But Frank Nixon could never make much money. In 1922, the family moved to the nearby town of Whittier, near Los Angeles. There Frank Nixon ran a gas station. Later he opened a grocery store. Unfortunately, he found little success in these business ventures. The family always struggled to make ends meet.

Richard was the second of five sons in the Nixon family. Shown here from left to right are Harold, Frank, Donald (on his mother's lap), Hannah, and Richard. The youngest boys, Arthur and Edward, had not yet been born when this photograph was taken.

Interesting Facts

▸ Richard Nixon was a descendant of James Nixon, who arrived in Delaware from Ireland in 1753. One of Richard's ancestors fought in the American Revolution. Another fought in the Civil War.

▸ Richard's father, Frank Nixon, never graduated from high school. When he was 12 years old, he had to find a job so he could help support his family.

▸ Hannah Nixon made sure the family went to church three times on Sunday and again on Wednesday evenings.

Richard Nixon first went to public school in Yorba Linda. He changed schools when his family moved to Whittier. As a boy, Richard had a terrible time getting along with his classmates because he was shy. He also became angry if he didn't get his way. Because he wasn't popular, Richard pushed himself to earn good grades. He was always smart and worked hard. He was among the best students in his class all through school.

Before Richard Nixon entered high school, tragedy struck the family. His little brother Arthur died. Two years later, his older brother, Harold, became sick with tuberculosis, a serious lung disease. This was an especially difficult time for Richard, who was very close to Harold. Hannah Nixon took care of Harold at home for a long time. Finally, she took him to live in Arizona, hoping the dry desert air would cure him. While she was away, the other Nixon sons helped their father run the household and the family business. She returned home two years later, in 1933, after Harold died.

By the time his mother returned to California, Richard had graduated from high

8

school and enrolled in Whittier College. There he continued to earn good grades. He also became a student leader and the president of his class.

After Richard graduated from college, he decided to become a lawyer. His parents did not have enough money to send him to law school, but his good grades earned him a scholarship, which would help him pay his **tuition** to Duke University Law School

Although he wasn't a natural athlete, Richard (back row, center) worked hard to succeed on the Whittier College football team. This photo was taken in 1933.

▸ Richard Nixon began working in his father's gas station and grocery store when he was still a boy. When he was a teenager, he woke up at 4 AM each day so he could stock the store's produce counter before he went to school.

▸ Richard Nixon's mother also attended Whittier College.

in Durham, North Carolina. He received his law degree in 1937 and returned to California. He went to work in a law office in Whittier. Soon he met a woman named Thelma Catherine Patricia Ryan. Pat, as she called herself, was a schoolteacher. In 1940, Pat Ryan and Richard Nixon were married.

Pat Ryan and Richard Nixon were married on June 21, 1940.

10

In 1942, the Nixons moved to Washington, D.C., after Richard was offered a position at the U.S. Office of Emergency Management. In the nation's capital city, he became increasingly interested in politics. Richard became a member of the Republican Party, one of the nation's two major **political parties.**

Even though he liked his new job, Richard left it after a few months. The United States had entered World War II in December of 1941. Richard decided he wanted to enter the military. He became an officer with the U.S. Navy and was sent to serve in the Pacific. He worked with the South Pacific Combat Air Transport Command and was in charge of the navy's airplanes. Nixon's leadership abilities helped him achieve success. By the end of the war, he had reached the important rank of lieutenant commander.

Nixon's leadership abilities helped him succeed in the U.S. Navy. He served in the South Pacific from 1942 until the end of World War II in 1945.

LIKE HER HUSBAND, THELMA "PAT" Nixon had a difficult childhood. Her family worked hard but never made much money. "I didn't know what it was not to work hard," she once said. But she remembered good times, too. "It was a good kind of life when you look back on it. I worked right along with my brothers in the fields, which was lots of fun," she recalled.

When Pat was 14, tragedy struck her family. Her mother died, leaving Pat to care for her father and brothers and to tend the house. Two years later, her father became ill. Pat took care of him until his death in 1930. Even with the extra work at home, Pat did very well in school. She dreamed of going to college and of making something of her life. "I wanted to start with an education," she recalled.

Working as a janitor to earn money for school, Pat enrolled at a community college. Then in 1931, an elderly couple asked her to help them move to the East Coast. Pat jumped at the chance to see another part of the country. Once there, she decided to stay in New York. She worked in a hospital until 1934, and then she returned to California and went back to college. After she graduated, Pat became a teacher at Whittier Union High School. Her students admired her friendly personality. She treated her students like adults and enjoyed her work.

In 1937, Pat tried out for a part in a play with the town's theater group. There she met Richard Nixon, who said that for him, "it was love at first sight." Pat wasn't as impressed with Richard at first, but he finally won her heart. They married in 1940.

Over the years, Pat Nixon helped her husband in his political career. When he ran in elections, she helped with his **campaign.** She always loved to travel, so she went with her husband on trips whenever she could. As first lady, she went with President Nixon to China. She also made trips by herself to Africa and South America. Mrs. Nixon was often praised for her role as a goodwill ambassador, someone who works to improve relations with other countries. Americans also admired her because she volunteered her time to good causes. She also encouraged others to volunteer. "You volunteer because you love your country, your people, and because it makes you feel good."

When Richard Nixon resigned from the presidency, Mrs. Nixon publicly supported him. "I have great faith in my husband," she said. "I happen to love him." After the resignation, she became a very private person, preferring a quiet life spent with her family.

"I don't know what history will say about me," Richard Nixon once said, "but I know it will say that Pat Nixon was truly a wonderful woman." Mrs. Nixon died on June 22, 1993.

Chapter Two

Early Political Career

Nixon rose to the rank of lieutenant commander during his time in the navy. But after the war, he was ready for a career change. He gladly took the opportunity to run for Congress.

When World War II ended, America's soldiers and sailors returned home. Nixon worked as a lawyer in the navy for a short time before he decided to change careers. The Republican Party needed a **candidate** to run for Congress in the election of 1946. Nixon decided he was ready for a new challenge. He and Mrs. Nixon returned to California. As the campaign for Congress began, their first child, Patricia (nicknamed Tricia), was born in February of 1946. Their second child, Julie, would be born a few years later, in 1948.

During his campaign, Richard showed voters that he was a conservative, someone who wanted the country to stay the same and not to experience great change. At that time in history, many Americans were afraid of

communism. They believed that communists, led by the Communist Party in the **Soviet Union**, planned to take over the world. Some people were especially worried that American citizens had joined the Communist Party. They feared these Americans would help the Soviet Union gain power. They might even be spies, giving away secrets to the enemy. Nixon claimed that his opponent, Jerry Voorhis, was a communist. It wasn't true, but this helped Nixon win the election with 60 percent of the vote.

After winning the election, the Nixons moved back to Washington, D.C. Communism was a very important topic in the capital city. Some members of Congress wanted to investigate those thought to be involved in communist, or "un-American," activities. To investigate people, Congress created the House Un-American Activities Committee. During the

ELECT

RICHARD M.
NIXON
WORLD WAR II VETERAN
YOUR
CONGRESSMAN

Nixon decided to run for the House of Representatives in 1946. He won that election, beginning a long career in politics that would lead to the presidency.

15

The Nixons' first daughter, Tricia, was born in 1946, shortly after Richard Nixon left the navy.

first year of Nixon's term, he was **appointed** to this committee. He led a special investigation on a government worker named Alger Hiss. Mr. Hiss had been accused of passing secret information to a communist spy named Whittaker Chambers. Many people believed Hiss was innocent, but Nixon was determined to prove that he had committed a crime. Because of Nixon's efforts, Hiss was found guilty and went to prison for five years.

The Hiss investigation made Nixon famous all over the country. He became known as a tough fighter who would do anything to win. In 1950, the Republican Party asked Nixon to run for election to the U.S. Senate. Republican leaders thought he was ready for more responsibility, even though he did not have as much political experience as most senators.

During his campaign for the Senate, Nixon accused his opponent, Helen Gahagan Douglas, of not being tough enough on communists. He said she did not support the

House Un-American Activities Committee. Nixon won the election. At 38 years old, he was the youngest senator at the time. More success was on the way.

Nixon had only been a senator for a year and a half when the Republican Party **nominated** General Dwight D. Eisenhower to run for president in the election of 1952. They chose Nixon to run for the office of vice president. They hoped he would bring in votes from Westerners and conservatives.

By nature, Eisenhower was a quiet, gentle man. He had earned a reputation as a smart and courageous general during World War II. In the election, he said few bad things about the current president, Harry S. Truman. He also refused to say negative things about his opponent from the Democratic Party, Adlai Stevenson. To win the election, Eisenhower relied on his good reputation and on his promise to end the Korean War. Two years earlier, President Truman had sent U.S. soldiers to fight in South Korea after it was invaded by North Korea. Most Americans wanted the soldiers to come home.

Interesting Facts

▸ When Nixon was investigating whether Alger Hiss had passed state secrets to a communist, he found evidence that had been hidden in a pumpkin on a farm!

If Eisenhower refused to insult his opponents, Nixon was more than willing to do so. Yet again, he accused Democratic opponents of not being tough enough on communists. He called Adlai Stevenson "cowardly."

But then, in the middle of the campaign, Nixon was accused of dishonesty. Reporters discovered that while he was a senator, Republicans in California gave Nixon money. A newspaper headline declared, "Secret Rich Men's Trust Fund Keeps Nixon in Style Far Beyond His Salary." Nixon went on television and admitted he had taken the money. But he explained why: His family could not afford to pay all the expenses he had as a senator. He had used the money to stay in touch with voters back in California. He also pointed out that as senator, he had not done any special favors for the donors. After the speech, Americans agreed Nixon had done nothing wrong. Other people advised Eisenhower to choose someone else to run as the vice-presidential candidate. Instead, when Nixon went to see him, Eisenhower said, "Dick, you're my boy."

Dwight Eisenhower and Richard Nixon easily won the election of 1952. When Eisen-

hower ran for reelection in 1956, he again chose Nixon as the vice-presidential candidate. Nixon served as vice president for a total of eight years.

American presidents often give vice presidents little to do, but Eisenhower was different. He asked Nixon to attend **cabinet** meetings. Nixon also attended meetings with military advisors. President Eisenhower kept Nixon up-to-date on what was happening in the nation. Nixon often helped Eisenhower make important decisions.

During Eisenhower's presidency, the United States became more and more involved in the Cold War, the growing feelings of distrust between the United States and the Soviet Union.

It seemed that a war could erupt at any time between the two nations. Nixon supported Eisenhower's decision to stockpile nuclear arms in case the Soviet Union ever attacked. These dangerous weapons were capable of terrible destruction.

Three times during Eisenhower's presidency, Nixon even assumed the president's duties. Eisenhower had many health problems that forced him to take time off. In 1955, he had a heart attack. In 1956, he had an operation. The following year, he had more health problems. During each of Eisenhower's illnesses, Nixon acted as the U.S. president.

In September of 1955, President Eisenhower had a heart attack while he was on vacation in Colorado. Richard Nixon took on the president's duties while Eisenhower recovered. By the following February, Eisenhower was well and announced his plans to run for reelection that year.

THE U.S. **CONSTITUTION** gives the vice president just two responsibilities: to **preside** over the Senate and to cast a ballot in a Senate vote in case of a tie. All vice presidents have fulfilled these duties. Some presidents have also given their vice presidents more to do. Richard Nixon would be one of the most active vice presidents up to that time.

In early American history, the Constitution said the vice president would be the person who came in second in a presidential election. But the 12th Amendment, passed in 1804, said that that a political party should include on its ticket one candidate for president and another for vice president. For a long time, many vice presidents devoted little time to the job. But when President William Henry Harrison died suddenly in office, his vice president, John Tyler, took over. Americans realized how important the job of vice president could suddenly become. Today vice presidents are often important politicians who run for the office of president when the president leaves office. In recent years, George Bush, Ronald Reagan's vice president, won election to the nation's highest office. Bill Clinton's vice president, Al Gore, ran in the election of 2000, but lost to George W. Bush, son of the former president.

21

Chapter THREE

President Nixon

In the 1960 presidential election, Nixon ran against a young senator from Massachusetts named John F. Kennedy (above).

IN 1960, THE REPUBLICAN PARTY NOMINATED Richard Nixon to run for president. The Democratic Party nominated John Fitzgerald Kennedy. In the beginning, Kennedy seemed unlikely to win. Many Americans thought he was too young to be president. But Kennedy gained support during the campaign and won the election by a very small number of votes. Out of more than 68 million votes cast, he received only 118,000 more than Nixon.

After Nixon's defeat, he and his family went back to California. There he returned to his work as a lawyer. Nixon missed politics, however, and decided to run for governor of California in 1962. He lost that election, too. It seemed as if his career in politics was over.

Interesting Facts

▶ While campaigning
for Barry Goldwater,
the Republican run-
ning for president
in 1964, Nixon
visited 36 states. In
1966, he visited 35
states while campaig-
ing for Republicans
running for election
to Congress.

During this period, the political situation
in the United States changed rapidly. When
President Kennedy was **assassinated** in 1963,
vice president Lyndon Baines Johnson became
president. At first, Johnson was a very popular
president. But during his second term, the
United States became more involved in the

Nixon was the favorite to win the election of 1968. He campaigned around the country, telling people that by voting for him, they were "voting to restore the respect for America."

Vietnam War. Communist North Vietnam was trying to take over its neighbor, South Vietnam. The U.S. government wanted to keep this from happening. But Americans began to doubt whether the country should be sending thousands of soldiers to fight communism in a country so far away. As Johnson continued to struggle with the Vietnam War, he became unpopular. He decided not to run for reelection in 1968. The Democrats nominated Johnson's vice president, Hubert Humphrey, instead. The Republicans chose Richard Nixon. During the campaign, Nixon appealed to conservatives, whom he called the Silent Majority. He said he believed the government wasted too much money. He promised to fight crime. He also promised to end **inflation.**

This was a very difficult time in the United States. Around the country, young people were waging **protests** against the Vietnam War. At marches and demonstrations, they displayed signs, chanted slogans, and gave speeches reflecting their belief that the United States should send no more soldiers to fight in the war. Sometimes protests turned violent when police or troops were called in to break them up.

Another source of turmoil in the United States was the **Civil Rights Movement.** For many years, civil rights leaders had been fighting for equal rights for African Americans. They had won some victories, but it was a difficult battle. On April 4, 1968, the Civil Rights Movement suffered a terrible blow when one of its most important leaders, Martin Luther King Jr., was assassinated. King had helped

▶ President Nixon believed that people were out to get him. He asked his staff to keep a list of his "enemies." This list included not only his political opponents, but also newspaper reporters, actors, athletes, and businesspeople.

▶ Singer Elvis Presley was a huge fan of President Nixon.

keep the movement peaceful, but violence broke out after his death. African Americans rioted across the United States.

Nixon disliked protesters, regardless of what they were fighting against. He believed these people did not respect their country. During his presidential campaign, he promised to bring "peace and order" back to the United States. He avoided talking about the Vietnam War, however. He said only that he would find an "honorable end" to it.

Richard Nixon won the election of 1968 and became president in January of 1969. From the beginning, he was a strong president. Always a loner by nature, he trusted only a few close advisors. He spent a great deal of time alone, reviewing documents and making plans.

President Nixon faced many problems. First, he worked to get the United States out of the Vietnam War. He asked that the government stop **drafting** young men into the military. He also decreased the number of American soldiers in Vietnam. Finally, he decided to end the war by secretly bombing Cambodia and Laos. The North Vietnamese

NIXON'S BOMBS KILL PEOPLE

army brought supplies in from these Asian countries. By bombing them, Nixon closed the supply routes. But the bombings also hurt many innocent people. When news of the bombings spread, new protests began. Many people believed Nixon was making the war bigger instead of ending it as he had promised. One protest ended in tragedy when National Guardsmen fired guns on protesters at Kent State University in Ohio. Four young students were killed.

Peace talks would eventually succeed, and the last American troops would leave Vietnam

Nixon hoped to end the Vietnam War more quickly, and he secretly ordered the bombing of Laos and Cambodia. Americans were furious about this, believing too many innocent lives had been lost. In response to criticism of his actions, Nixon said, "Those who have power are seldom popular."

27

in 1973. By this time, Nixon had realized that one way to end the war completely was to work with powerful communist countries, such as China and the Soviet Union. These nations supported North Vietnam, so Nixon made an historic visit to China. This opened relations between that country and the United States. Nixon then became the first U.S. president ever to visit the Soviet Union. It began to seem possible that one day, the two countries might not be enemies.

Foreign affairs had taken up most of Nixon's attention during his first term, but he did help the United States as well. He pushed Congress to pass anticrime laws. He established a new program to protect the environment. He also supported NASA's space program.

On July 20, 1969, President Nixon held an historic telephone conversation in the Oval Office when he talked to astronauts on the moon.

In 1969, Americans rejoiced when the United States sent astronauts to the moon in a rocket. The entire country stopped to watch Neil Armstrong walk on the moon.

In 1972, Nixon ran for reelection. His opponent was Democratic Senator George McGovern. In the campaign, Nixon mostly talked about how proud he was to have brought the American soldiers home from Vietnam. He won the election by a landslide.

Interesting Facts

▶ Environmentalists organized the first Earth Day on April 22, 1970, during Nixon's first term. All over the country, people gave speeches about protecting the environment and fighting pollution.

IN 1972, RICHARD NIXON MADE HISTORY WHEN HE VISITED THE PEOPLE'S Republic of China. In the 1950s, the United States and China had a poor relationship because China was a communist country. The United States had worked to prevent China from joining the United Nations, an international organization that works for world peace. The U.S. had also refused to trade with China. The United States did not buy goods made in China and refused to sell American goods there. It asked other **democracies** to do the same.

But in 1969, Richard Nixon wanted to build better relations with China. At the time, Chinese leaders were concerned that the Soviet Union might try to invade Asia. They hoped the United States would help prevent this. In 1970, Nixon expressed interest in visiting China. The next spring, members of an American ping-pong team became the first Americans in many years to go there. In June, Secretary of State Henry Kissinger, who was one of Nixon's aides, went to Beijing to meet with Chinese leaders. Together they made plans for Nixon to visit.

Richard and Pat Nixon arrived in China on February 22, 1972. Reporters and television camera crews went with them. President Nixon's walk on the Great Wall and his meetings with Chinese leaders were televised. Americans expressed great interest in the country. They admired its beautiful scenery and exotic animals. They were proud of Nixon and hoped that soon the world might become a more peaceful place. "I'm the president that opened relations with China after 25 years of no communication," Nixon once said. His visit to China was one of his most important achievements.

Chapter FOUR

Nixon Resigns

Nixon had a number of successes while he was in office, but acts of dishonesty would soon overshadow his achievements.

AT THE BEGINNING OF HIS SECOND TERM, Nixon worked to cut the government's spending on **welfare,** education, and law enforcement. Cities and states began to share more of these expenses, rather than depending on the national government. To fight inflation, Nixon ordered a price freeze. Companies could not raise prices on their products for a certain period of time. He also placed a tax on foreign goods to encourage Americans to buy things that were made in the United States. He continued his interest in foreign affairs.

But soon, most of President Nixon's time was taken up with serious problems. First, his vice president, Spiro T. Agnew, had been accused of dishonesty. Agnew was forced to resign in 1973, and Gerald R. Ford replaced

him as vice president. Soon the nation discovered that Nixon himself was involved in illegal activities. Americans learned of his part in the Watergate **scandal.**

While Richard Nixon was running for reelection in 1972, Republicans played "dirty tricks" on the Democrats to help him win. For one thing, the Republican Committee for the Reelection of the President used illegal gifts of money to find out what the Democrats were planning. They also organized a burglary. The Democratic Party had its national headquarters in a hotel in Washington, D.C., called the Watergate.

Although the Watergate scandal took up much of President Nixon's time during 1974, he continued to work for better relations with other countries. He is shown here with Soviet leader Leonid Brezhnev (right) after the signing of a treaty.

President Nixon's advisors hired five men to break into the Democrats' office. Once inside, they hoped to steal information about their opponents' campaign plans. They also planned to place a device in the office that would allow them to listen to the Democrats' phone calls. Nixon's aides hoped this would help him win reelection.

The burglary took place in June of 1972, but it was not a success. The burglars were arrested at the scene of the crime. They would later be tried and sent to prison. For a time, Americans believed President Nixon when he said that he knew nothing about the burglary. They soon lost trust in him, however. The public learned that even if Nixon did not plan the theft, he had to have known about it. Nixon tried to cover it up, or hide the truth. He did not want Americans to find out about his role in the scandal.

When rumors of the cover-up reached the Senate, its members appointed investigators to look into the matter. Although Nixon and his aides lied when they answered questions, the investigators found out that Nixon had used tape recorders in his office.

Nixon had recorded all the conversations held there. The investigators pressed the president to give them the tapes of his conversations about the Watergate scandal. In April of 1974, Nixon released **transcripts** of the tapes, but some information had been removed. Nixon did not want to release the tapes themselves, but the **Supreme Court** ordered him to do so a few months later, on July 24.

The tapes proved that President Nixon knew about the Watergate burglary. Even worse, they proved that Nixon had ordered the cover-up. When members of Congress realized Nixon had covered up the crime, he lost all support. Even his oldest political friends refused to help him. Congress wanted to impeach the president.

President Nixon released transcripts of his taped conversations on April 29, 1974. By July, the Supreme Court had ordered him to give up the tapes themselves.

Nixon's family stood by him during the Watergate scandal. He is shown here with his daughters, Tricia (left) and Julie, and his son-in-law, Edward Cox. During his resignation speech, the president told Americans he was sorry to leave the presidency but that he believed it was the best thing for the country. "I would say only that if some of my judgments were wrong—and some were wrong—they were made in what I believed at the time to be the best interests of the nation."

This meant he would face a trial in the Senate.

Nixon knew that if he were impeached, he would almost certainly be found guilty and forced to step down from the presidency. Before impeachment proceedings could begin, President Nixon resigned. He announced his decision to the nation on August 8, 1974.

One day later, his family boarded a helicopter on the White House lawn and flew home to California. That same day, Gerald Ford was sworn in as the new president. Ford soon **pardoned** Nixon for any crime he had committed. This meant Nixon could not be tried in a court of law or sent to prison.

Richard Nixon lived for 20 years after he resigned from the presidency. He never again held an official government job, and most Americans considered him to be dishonest. Over time, however, some opinions changed. Nixon became a respected **statesman.** He gave speeches and wrote books about foreign affairs. He offered advice about U.S. relations with other countries. He also traveled around the world to meet with foreign leaders. Later presidents telephoned Nixon or invited him to the White House to ask his opinion.

In recent years, books about Richard Nixon have criticized him for Watergate. But they have also praised him for his achievements as a statesman. On April 22, 1994, shortly after a final trip to the Soviet Union and completing his 11th book, Richard Nixon died at the age of 81.

Interesting Facts

▸ The first president to be impeached was Andrew Johnson, who found himself in trouble after he fired a government official. Congress said that this was not Johnson's right and that he had committed a crime in doing so.

▸ The only other president to be impeached was William (Bill) Clinton, who faced impeachment hearings in 1998.

Nixon made plans to establish his presidential library. It opened in Yorba Linda in 1990. President George Bush (far left) and former presidents (from left to right) Ronald Reagan, Jimmy Carter, and Gerald Ford attended the dedication ceremony.

1913 Richard Milhous Nixon is born on January 9 in Yorba Linda, California.

1922 The Nixon family moves from Yorba Linda to the nearby town of Whittier, where Frank Nixon opens a gas station.

1930 Nixon graduates from high school and enrolls at Whittier College.

1937 Nixon graduates from the law school at Duke University and begins his career as an attorney.

1940 Richard Nixon marries Pat Ryan.

1942 Nixon is appointed an attorney for the U.S. Office of Emergency Management. He and Pat move to Washington, D.C. Within a few months, he leaves his job to join the navy.

1946 The Nixons have their first child, a daughter named Patricia. Nixon is elected to the U.S. House of Representatives.

1948 Julie, the Nixons second daughter, is born.

1950 Nixon runs for election to the Senate and wins.

1952 Dwight Eisenhower runs for president with Nixon as the vice-presidential candidate. Nixon is accused of accepting money and gifts from wealthy Republicans. He appears on national television, saying that he only took money to help pay his campaign expenses. Eisenhower and Nixon win the election.

1955 Richard Nixon assumes the president's responsibilities when Eisenhower becomes sick.

1956 Eisenhower and Nixon are reelected.

1960 Richard Nixon runs for election as president but loses to John F. Kennedy.

1962 Nixon loses the election for governor of California.

1963 President Kennedy is assassinated on November 22. Vice President Lyndon Baines Johnson becomes president.

1968 Civil Rights Movement leader Martin Luther King Jr. is assassinated on April 4, leading to violent protests. Nixon is elected president of the United States in November.

1969 On July 20, *Apollo 11* astronaut Neil Armstrong becomes the first person to walk on the moon, winning the "space race" for the United States. Millions of people around the world watch the moon landing on television.

1970 Environmentalists organize the first Earth Day on April 22. Nixon secretly bombs North Vietnam's supply routes in Cambodia and Laos, killing many innocent people. On May 4, four students are killed during an antiwar protest at Kent State University in Ohio.

1971 Nixon announces that he will visit the People's Republic of China, stunning the world because he had long been firmly opposed to communism. The Nixons' daughter Tricia marries Edward Cox at the White House.

1972 Nixon visits China in February, opening relations between the two countries for the first time since China became a communist country in 1949. In May, Nixon becomes the first U.S. president to visit the Soviet Union. In June, burglars break into Democratic Party headquarters to steal information to help Nixon win reelection. When the burglars are caught, Nixon and other officials try to cover up their involvement in the scandal. Nixon wins the election in November, defeating Democrat George McGovern.

1973 The last American troops leave Vietnam. Americans learn about the Watergate scandal.

1974 Throughout the winter and spring, Congress investigates Nixon's involvement in the Watergate burglary. Nixon avoids giving information to investigators. In April, he releases edited transcripts of his conversations in the Oval Office, but much of the information has been removed. On July 24, the Supreme Court rules that Nixon must turn over all the tapes. On August 5, he releases tapes that prove he knew about the burglary and that he tried to cover it up. On August 8, Richard Nixon announces to the American people that he will resign. Gerald Ford is sworn in as the new president on August 9. Ford pardons Nixon in September.

1990 The Nixon presidential library opens. Richard Nixon is honored when four other presidents attend the ceremony.

1993 Pat Nixon dies on June 22.

1994 Richard Nixon dies on April 22.

Glossary Terms

appointed (uh-POINT-ed)
When someone is appointed, he or she is asked by an important official to accept a position. Nixon was appointed to the House Un-American Activities Committee.

assassinate (uh-SASS-ih-nayt)
Assassinate means to murder someone, especially a well-known person. President Kennedy was assassinated in 1963.

cabinet (KAB-ih-net)
A cabinet is the group of people who advise a president. President Eisenhower invited Nixon to attend cabinet meetings.

campaign (kam-PAYN)
A campaign is the process of running for an election, including activities such as giving speeches or attending rallies. Pat Nixon helped with her husband's campaigns.

candidate (KAN-dih-det)
A candidate is a person running in an election. The Republican Party asked Nixon to become a candidate in the 1946 election for Congress.

**Civil Rights Movement
(SIV-el RYTZ MOOV-ment)**
The Civil Rights Movement was the struggle for equal rights for African Americans in the United States during the 1950s and 1960s. Martin Luther King Jr. was an important leader of the Civil Rights Movement.

communism (KOM-yeh-niz-em)
Communism is a system of government in which the central government, not the people, holds all the power. Many Americans were afraid of communism after World War II.

constitution (kon-stih-TOO-shun)
A constitution is the set of basic principles that govern a country. The U.S. Constitution describes the duties of the nation's leaders.

democracies (deh-MOK-ruh-seez)
Democracies are nations in which the people control the government by electing their own leaders. The United States is a democracy.

draft (DRAFT)
When people are drafted, they are required to serve in the armed forces. President Nixon asked the government to stop drafting men into the military in an attempt to stop the Vietnam War.

inflation (in-FLAY-shun)
Inflation is a sharp and sudden rise in the price of goods. During his 1968 campaign, Nixon promised to end inflation in the United States.

nominate (NOM-ih-nayt)
If a political party nominates someone, it chooses that person to run for a political office. The Republican Party nominated Nixon to run for president in the 1968 election.

pardon (PAR-don)
If a leader pardons someone, he or she excuses that person for crimes or misdeeds. President Gerald Ford pardoned Richard Nixon.

**political parties
(puh-LIT-ih-kul PAR-teez)**
Political parties are groups of people who share similar ideas about how to run a government. Nixon was a member of the Republican political party.

preside (pre-ZYD)
If someone presides over a meeting, he or she is in charge of it. The vice president presides over sessions in the Senate.

protests (PROH-tests)
Protests are gatherings at which people speak out against something they believe is wrong. In the 1960s, many young people took part in protests against the Vietnam War.

resign (ree-ZINE)
When a person resigns from a job, he or she gives it up. Nixon was the first president of the United States to resign from office.

scandal (SKAN-dul)
A scandal is a shameful action that shocks the public. The Watergate scandal involved President Nixon.

Soviet Union (SOH-vee-et YOON-yen)
The Soviet Union was a communist country that stretched from eastern Europe across Asia to the Pacific Ocean. It separated into several smaller countries in 1991.

statesman (STAYTS-man)
A statesman is a person skilled at managing public or national affairs. Some people considered Nixon a respected statesman.

**Supreme Court
(suh-PREEM KORT)**
The Supreme Court is the highest court in the United States. The Supreme Court ruled that President Nixon had to turn over the tapes from the Oval Office conversations.

transcripts (TRAN-skriptz)
Transcripts are written records of what was said in a conversation or interview. Nixon released transcripts of the taped Watergate scandal conversations in 1974.

tuition (too-ISH-un)
Tuition is the fee for going to a school. Nixon's good grades earned him a scholarship, which helped pay his tuition to law school.

welfare (WELL-fair)
Welfare is aid provided by the government to people in need. Nixon reduced government spending on welfare programs.

Our PRESIDENTS

President	Birthplace	Life Span	Presidency	Political Party	First Lady
George Washington	Virginia	1732–1799	1789–1797	None	Martha Dandridge Custis Washington
John Adams	Massachusetts	1735–1826	1797–1801	Federalist	Abigail Smith Adams
Thomas Jefferson	Virginia	1743–1826	1801–1809	Democratic-Republican	widower
James Madison	Virginia	1751–1836	1809–1817	Democratic Republican	Dolley Payne Todd Madison
James Monroe	Virginia	1758–1831	1817–1825	Democratic Republican	Elizabeth Kortright Monroe
John Quincy Adams	Massachusetts	1767–1848	1825–1829	Democratic-Republican	Louisa Johnson Adams
Andrew Jackson	South Carolina	1767–1845	1829–1837	Democrat	widower
Martin Van Buren	New York	1782–1862	1837–1841	Democrat	widower
William H. Harrison	Virginia	1773–1841	1841	Whig	Anna Symmes Harrison
John Tyler	Virginia	1790–1862	1841–1845	Whig	Letitia Christian Tyler / Julia Gardiner Tyler
James K. Polk	North Carolina	1795–1849	1845–1849	Democrat	Sarah Childress Polk

Our PRESIDENTS

President	Birthplace	Life Span	Presidency	Political Party	First Lady
Zachary Taylor	Virginia	1784–1850	1849–1850	Whig	Margaret Mackall Smith Taylor
Millard Fillmore	New York	1800–1874	1850–1853	Whig	Abigail Powers Fillmore
Franklin Pierce	New Hampshire	1804–1869	1853–1857	Democrat	Jane Means Appleton Pierce
James Buchanan	Pennsylvania	1791–1868	1857–1861	Democrat	never married
Abraham Lincoln	Kentucky	1809–1865	1861–1865	Republican	Mary Todd Lincoln
Andrew Johnson	North Carolina	1808–1875	1865–1869	Democrat	Eliza McCardle Johnson
Ulysses S. Grant	Ohio	1822–1885	1869–1877	Republican	Julia Dent Grant
Rutherford B. Hayes	Ohio	1822–1893	1877–1881	Republican	Lucy Webb Hayes
James A. Garfield	Ohio	1831–1881	1881	Republican	Lucretia Rudolph Garfield
Chester A. Arthur	Vermont	1829–1886	1881–1885	Republican	widower
Grover Cleveland	New Jersey	1837–1908	1885–1889	Democrat	Frances Folsom Cleveland

Our PRESIDENTS

President	Birthplace	Life Span	Presidency	Political Party	First Lady
Benjamin Harrison	Ohio	1833–1901	1889–1893	Republican	Caroline Scott Harrison
Grover Cleveland	New Jersey	1837–1908	1893–1897	Democrat	Frances Folsom Cleveland
William McKinley	Ohio	1843–1901	1897–1901	Republican	Ida Saxton McKinley
Theodore Roosevelt	New York	1858–1919	1901–1909	Republican	Edith Kermit Carow Roosevelt
William H. Taft	Ohio	1857–1930	1909–1913	Republican	Helen Herron Taft
Woodrow Wilson	Virginia	1856–1924	1913–1921	Democrat	Ellen L. Axson Wilson Edith Bolling Galt Wilson
Warren G. Harding	Ohio	1865–1923	1921–1923	Republican	Florence Kling De Wolfe Harding
Calvin Coolidge	Vermont	1872–1933	1923–1929	Republican	Grace Goodhue Coolidge
Herbert C. Hoover	Iowa	1874–1964	1929–1933	Republican	Lou Henry Hoover
Franklin D. Roosevelt	New York	1882–1945	1933–1945	Democrat	Anna Eleanor Roosevelt Roosevelt
Harry S. Truman	Missouri	1884–1972	1945–1953	Democrat	Elizabeth Wallace Truman

44

Our PRESIDENTS

President	Birthplace	Life Span	Presidency	Political Party	First Lady
Dwight D. Eisenhower	Texas	1890–1969	1953–1961	Republican	Mary "Mamie" Doud Eisenhower
John F. Kennedy	Massachusetts	1917–1963	1961–1963	Democrat	Jacqueline Bouvier Kennedy
Lyndon B. Johnson	Texas	1908–1973	1963–1969	Democrat	Claudia Alta Taylor Johnson
Richard M. Nixon	California	1913–1994	1969–1974	Republican	Thelma Catherine Ryan Nixon
Gerald Ford	Nebraska	1913–	1974–1977	Republican	Elizabeth "Betty" Bloomer Warren Ford
James Carter	Georgia	1924–	1977–1981	Democrat	Rosalynn Smith Carter
Ronald Reagan	Illinois	1911–	1981–1989	Republican	Nancy Davis Reagan
George Bush	Massachusetts	1924–	1989–1993	Republican	Barbara Pierce Bush
William Clinton	Arkansas	1946–	1993–2001	Democrat	Hillary Rodham Clinton
George W. Bush	Connecticut	1946–	2001–	Republican	Laura Welch Bush

Presidential FACTS

Qualifications
To run for president, a candidate must
- be at least 35 years old
- be a citizen who was born in the United States
- have lived in the United States for 14 years

Term of Office
A president's term of office is four years. No president can stay in office for more than two terms.

Election Date
The presidential election takes place every four years on the first Tuesday of November.

Inauguration Date
Presidents are inaugurated on January 20.

Oath of Office
I do solemnly swear I will faithfully execute the office of the President of the United States and will to the best of my ability preserve, protect, and defend the Constitution of the United States.

Write a Letter to the President
One of the best things about being a U.S. citizen is that Americans get to participate in their government. They can speak out if they feel government leaders aren't doing their jobs. They can also praise leaders who are going the extra mile. Do you have something you'd like the president to do? Should the president worry more about the environment and encourage people to recycle? Should the government spend more money on our schools? You can write a letter to the president to say how you feel!

1600 Pennsylvania Avenue
Washington, D.C. 20500

You can even send an e-mail to: president@whitehouse.gov

46

For Further INFORMATION

Internet Sites

Visit the Nixon Library and birthplace:
http://www.nixonfoundation.org/

Read a biography about Pat Nixon:
http://www.nixonfoundation.org/TheNixons/PatNixon.shtml#TopOfPage

Listen to several of Richard Nixon's speeches:
http://www.webcorp.com/sounds/nixonarchive.htm

Read biographies about Richard Nixon:
http://www.unitedstates-on-line.com/Nixon37.html
http://www.ipl.org/ref/POTUS/rmnixon.html

Learn more about all the presidents and visit the White House:
http://www.whitehouse.gov/WH/glimpse/presidents/html/presidents.html
http://www.thepresidency.org/presinfo.htm
http://www.americanpresidents.org/

Books

Dudley, Mark E. *United States v. Nixon: Presidential Powers.* New York: Twenty First Century Books, 1995.

Feinberg, Barbara Silberdick. *Patricia Ryan Nixon: 1912–1993* (Encyclopedia of First Ladies). Chicago: Childrens Press, 1998.

Francis, Sandra. *Gerald R. Ford: Our Thirty-Eighth President.* Chanhassen, MN: The Child's World, 2002.

Fremon, David K. *The Watergate Scandal in American History* (In American History). Springfield, NJ: Enslow Publishers, 1996.

Galt, Margot Fortunato. *Stop This War: American Protest of the Conflict in Vietnam* (People's History). Minneapolis, MN: Lerner Publishing Group, 2000.

Morin, Isobel V. *Impeaching the President.* Brookfield, CT: Millbrook Press. 1996.

Index